A GIFT FOR

_____

FROM

_____

NO LIMITS BUT THE SKY

Copyright © 2002
Hallmark Licensing, Inc.

Published by Hallmark Books, a division of Hallmark Cards, Inc.,
Kansas City, MO 64141. www.hallmark.com.

Literary development, photography, and design production by
Koechel Peterson & Associates, Minneapolis, MN.

Contributing writers and editors : Ben Accardi, Eva Allen, Kay
Andrew, Derrick Barnes, Linda Barnes, Ellen Brenneman, Dorothy
Colgan, Ed Cunningham, Renee Duvall, Linda Elrod, Steve Finken,
Tina Hacker, Carolyn Hoppe, Jim Howard, Jeannie Hund, Ginnie
Job, Lisa Langford, Mary Loberg, Barbara Loots, Linda Staten,
Sharon Valleau, Molly Wigand

Printed and bound in China

BOK 5046

No Limits But the Sky

GIFT BOOKS
from Hallmark

Today's achievement marks . . .

a fond farewell to yesterday,

a warm welcome to tomorrow.

the sunset of a beautiful part of the past,

the sunrise of a bright new future.

the beginning of new challenges,

the promise of success in the future,

and the anticipation of ever greater happiness.

The future opens up before you

like a new book . . .

waiting for you

to commit to its pages

the story only you can write.

". . . and the hats whirled skyward,

buoyed by bright, new hopes

and propelled by big daring dreams!"

the beat of a heart

the fall of a sigh

the rise of a prayer—

the flash of a star

through limitless sky

the dreams that we dare.

celebrate life!

Reach for a Star

When we ponder the stars,

when we reach for our dreams,

we're never bothered

by how far away they seem.

Instead, we are inspired

by the beauty of our vision.

Dreams are like stars—brilliant and permanent.

Attempt the Impossible

To achieve all that is possible,

you must attempt the impossible.

To be as much as you can be,

you must dream of being more.

Your dream is the promise

of all you can become.

It is in dreaming the greatest dreams . . .

seeking the highest goals . . .

that we build the brightest tomorrows.

Tomorrows are only todays

waiting to happen.

What's in Yours?

Dreams are the greatest gift—

unwrap your future!

Stretch Your Dreams

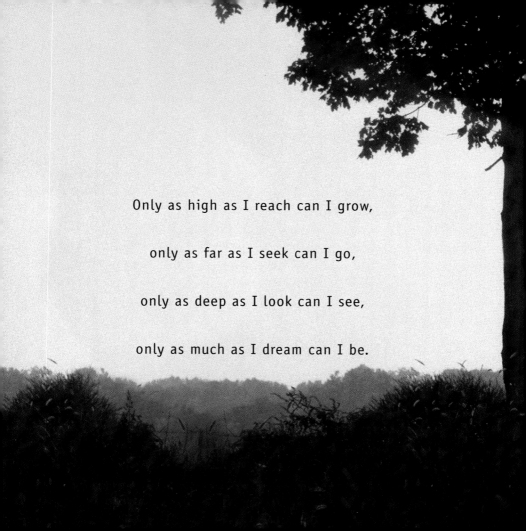

Only as high as I reach can I grow,

only as far as I seek can I go,

only as deep as I look can I see,

only as much as I dream can I be.

The Power Within

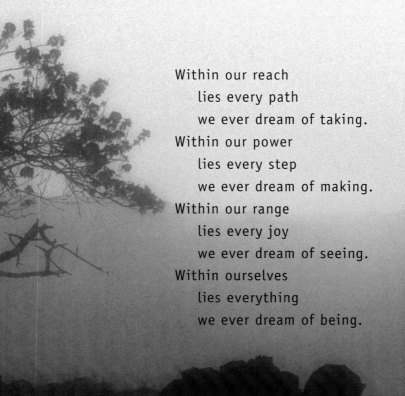

Within our reach
    lies every path
    we ever dream of taking.
Within our power
    lies every step
    we ever dream of making.
Within our range
    lies every joy
    we ever dream of seeing.
Within ourselves
    lies everything
    we ever dream of being.

DREAM

MAKERS

One dream becomes real . . .

a thousand dreams become possible.

I wish, I wish that I could know

the places I have yet to go,

the ways I'll change, the things I'll do,

the special dreams I'll make come true.

I wish, I wish that I could see

the life that lies ahead of me.

Embrace Your Dreams

Fall in love with life!

Embrace your dreams with passion!

Look beyond where others have been

to see where you would go.

DARE

"Let's dare to think some bold,

new thoughts,

trust life a little more,

unlearn some things that we've been taught.

Let's spread our wings and soar."

BE DIFFERENT!

To make a difference in the world,

you must first dare to be different.

When the truth needs to be said,

when the work needs to be done,

when the help needs to be given . . .

you can make a difference.

Do the Undo-Able

play it safe?

walk on the sidewalk?

drink your milk?

get lots and lots of z-z-z's?

or s-t-r-e-t-c-h that brain!

free that creativity!

dare to be different!

dare to strike out!

dare to do the undo-able!

after all,

maybe it's just been

undo-able

until YOU.

Look your chances in the eye—
it's "you" you have to satisfy!
You can never dream too big
or set your sights too high!

If they say you can't,
if they say you're not strong enough,
if they say no one has ever done it before,
you always say . . .
Just watch!

LAUNCH OUT

One doesn't discover new lands

without consenting to lose sight of the shore

for a very long time.

ANDRÉ GIDE

Say "Yes" to Life

Always laugh as much as possible

and cry a little less.

Conceive the inconceivable

and dare to tell Life, "Yes!"

Make the Discovery

The future doesn't lie ahead of you,

waiting to happen.

It lies deep inside of you,

waiting to be discovered.

So invite the unexpected.

It won't care if you're not the perfect host.

My spirit takes flight—

I am fearless and free

to express,

to explore,

to begin . . .

to be me.

Take the Brush

Your future

is an empty canvas

just waiting

for that first stroke.

Take Hold of Today

Make this your moment—

your time in the sun,

your chance to do something

that you've never done.

Forget about "should haves"

and "might haves" and "could haves."

Reach out and take hold of today!

Maybe good things come

to those who wait,

but the best things come

to those who seize the moment

and make it their own.

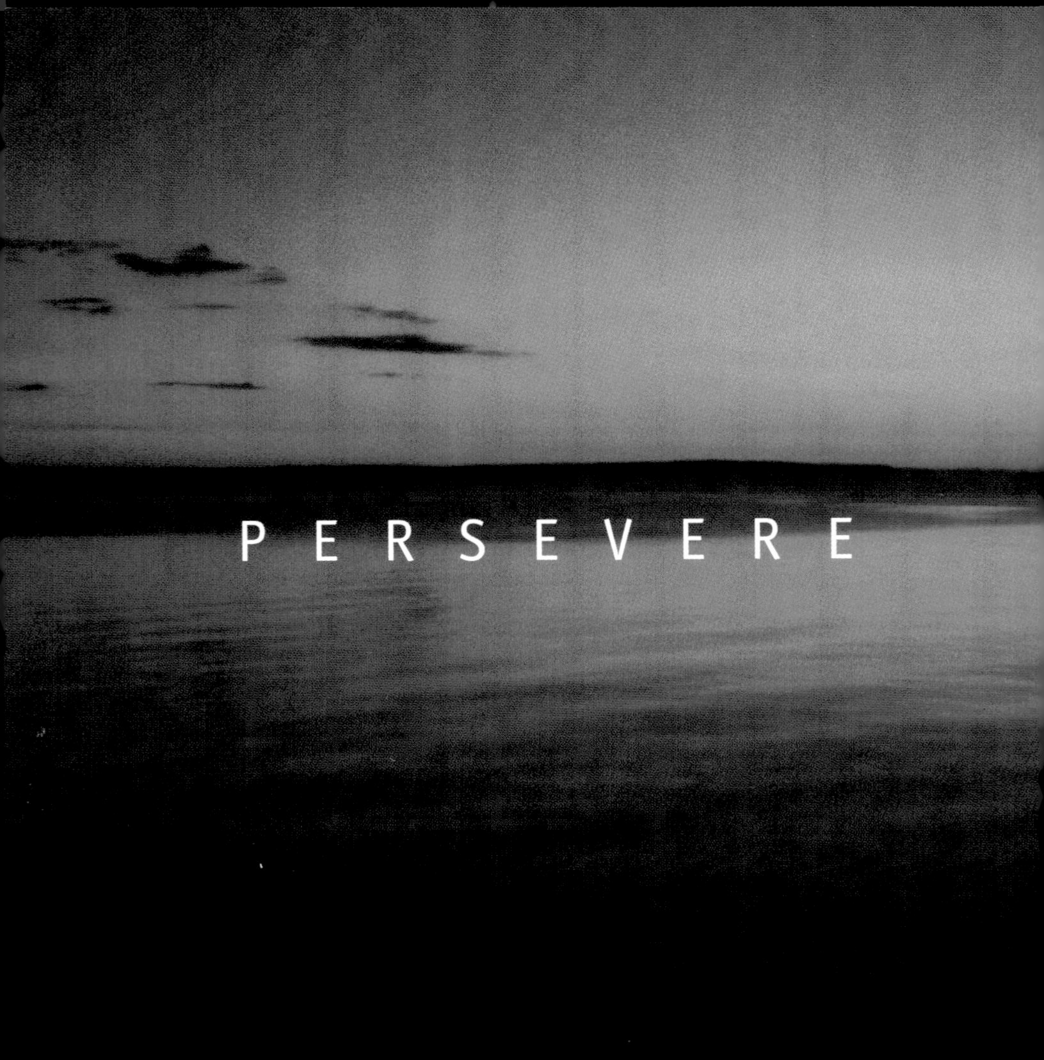
PERSEVERE

" . . . and so they set sail

for the Land of Possibility

where anything could happen,

and often did."

One foot in front of the other.

One dream. One horizon. Don't stop.

One path. Only one who can know it.

One you. On your way to the top.

There is nothing beyond the reach of you.

BE COURAGEOUS

Courage uncovers strength,

grace reveals beauty,

time strips away the frivolous,

life layers on experience,

and you have become

magnificent.

It is in meeting

the small challenges of daily living

that we prepare ourselves

for the great challenges of life.

Follow your dream . . .
take one step at a time
and don't settle for less,
just continue to climb.
Follow your dream . . .
if you stumble, don't stop
and lose sight of your goal,
press on to the top.
For only on top
can we see the whole view,
can we see what we've done
and what we can do,
can we then have the vision
to seek something new. . . .
Press on,
and follow your dream.

The Power

It is yours,

the challenge of life . . .

with your heart, hand, and mind

you hold the power to mold

each golden moment,

each shining hour

into new designs,

infinite possibilities.

Live Today

Cherish your yesterdays,

dream your tomorrows,

but live your todays.

Tomorrow belongs to those

who fully use today.

Reach the Sky

Climb high,

climb far,

your goal the sky,

your aim the star.

Perseverance is the investment.

Success is the return.

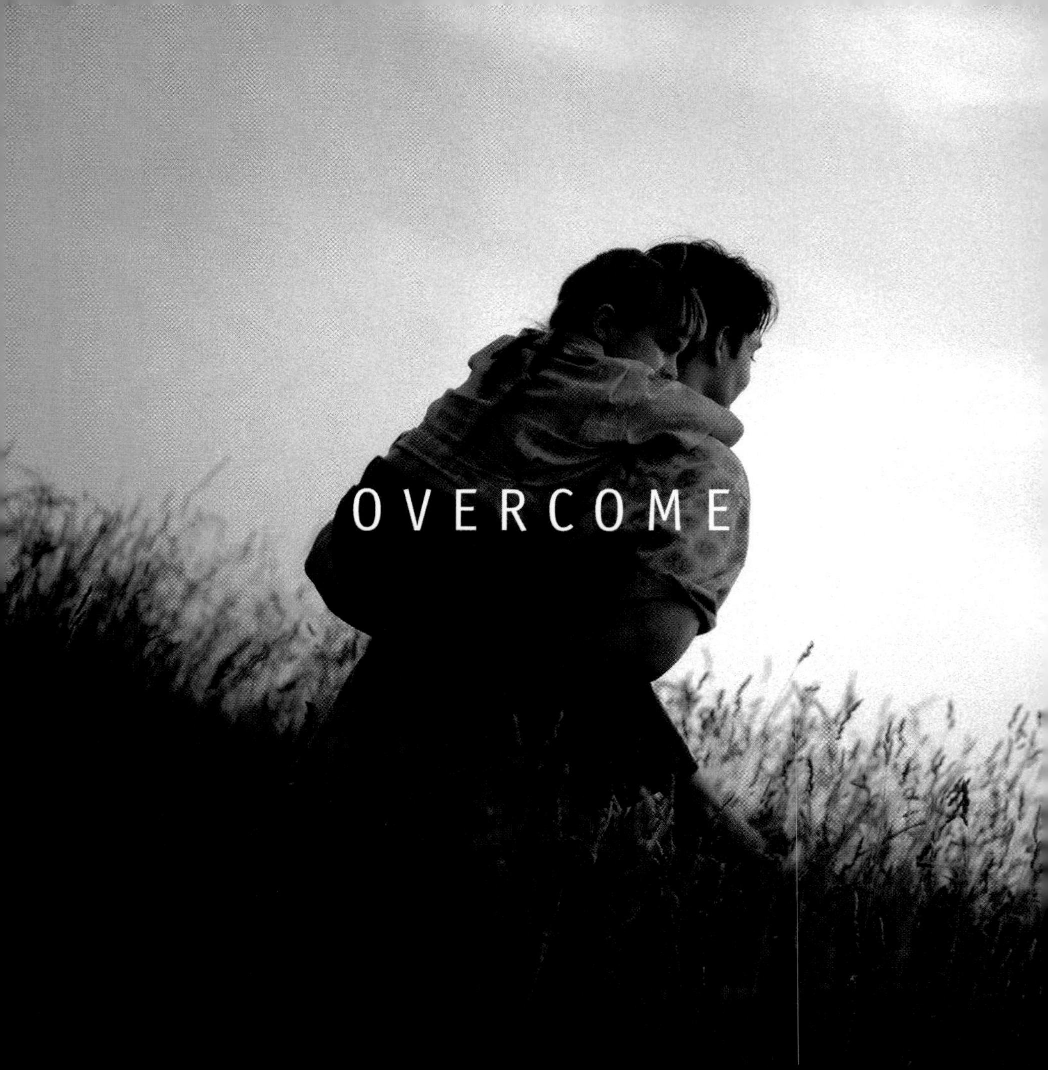
OVERCOME

I have learned that success

is to be measured

not so much by the position

that one has reached in life

as by the obstacles

which he has overcome

while trying to succeed.

BOOKER T. WASHINGTON

Joy in the Journey

There was a time I seemed to sail

upon a vast, blue sea,

scanning the horizon

for some distant, golden shore,

imagining that happiness

lay just ahead of me

in some wondrous, perfect place

I'd never seen before. . . .

But as the days and years passed by,

I came to comprehend

that joy is in the journeying,

not at the journey's end.

SUCCEED

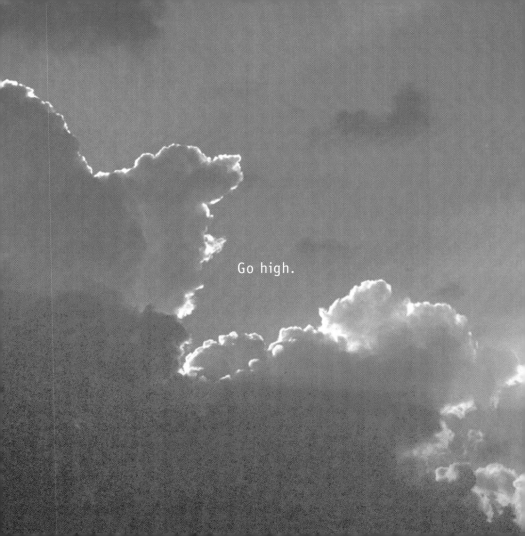

Being You

To live your life in your own way . . .

to reach for the goals you have set for yourself . . .

to be the you that you want to be—

that is success.

Let success be measured

by the happiness in your heart.

Even as we dream,

we begin to succeed...

even as we succeed,

we begin to dream again.

Do What You Love

Do what you love,

and it will make your soul rich.

Do what you'd do

if you knew every dream

could come true.

When you're doing what you love,

it feels as if you're flying.

The Secret

Behind every success

is endeavor . . .

Behind endeavor,

ability . . .

Behind ability,

knowledge . . .

Behind knowledge,

a seeker.

Do Your Best

What could be more important in life

than to know in our hearts that in everything

we have tried to do,

we have done our very best.

The courage of conviction,

the strength to persevere,

the hope that survives disappointment—

these are the keys to success.

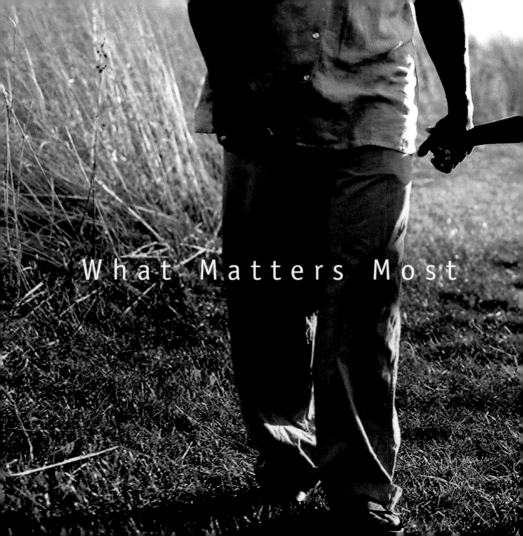

What Matters Most

Success lies not in how well-known you are,

but how well-respected . . .

not in your power to take,

but your willingness to give.

It is measured

by the height of your aspirations,

the breadth of your vision,

the depth of your convictions.

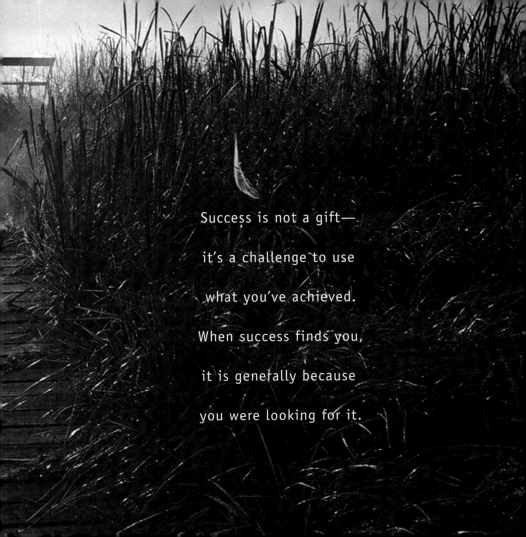

Success is not a gift—

it's a challenge to use

what you've achieved.

When success finds you,

it is generally because

you were looking for it.

What I Leave Behind

I hope my achievements in life shall be these—

that I will have fought for what was right and fair,

that I will have risked for that which mattered,

that I will have given help to those who were in need...

that I will have left the earth a better place

for what I've done and who I've been.

Don't forget to glance up from your keyboard
and see how blue the sky is now and then.

Don't forget to put away your cell phone
and spend some time alone with paintbrush or pen.

Don't forget to seek the sound of silence
and let the daily traffic rush on by.

Remember that the secret of success is
how happily you climb and not how high.